WILDLIFE VIEWING AREAS

1. Komodo National Park
2. Sepilok Forest Reserve
3. Danum Valley Conservation Area
4. Mount Mulu National Park
5. Mount Leuser National Park
6. Kericini-Seblat National Park
7. Ujung Kulon National Park
8. Tonle Sap Great Lake
9. Hlawaga National Park
10. Mount Victoria National Park
11. Hala-Bala Wildlife Sanctuary
12. Tabin Wildlife Reserve
13. Doi Inthanon National Park
14. Thungyai Naresuan Wildlife Sanctuary
15. Phu Wua Wildlife Sanctuary
16. Way Kambas National Park
17. Tangkoko Nature Reserve
18. Cuc Phuong National Park
19. Phong Nha-Ke Bang National Park
20. Philippine Tarsier and Wildlife Sanctuary
21. Pamilican Island
22. St. Paul's Subterranean River National Park
23. Sabangau National Park
24. Kuala Gandah Elephant Sanctuary

Text & illustrations © 2015, 2023 Waterford Press Inc. All rights reserved. Photos © Shutterstock. To order or for information on custom published products please call 800-434-2555 or email orderdesk@waterfordpress.com. For permissions or to share comments email editor@waterfordpress.com. 2301431

$7.95 U.S.
$9.95 CAN

ISBN 978-1-58355-962-8

50795

9 781583 559628

8 44682 01110 9

10 9 8 7 6 5 4 3 2 1

Made in the USA

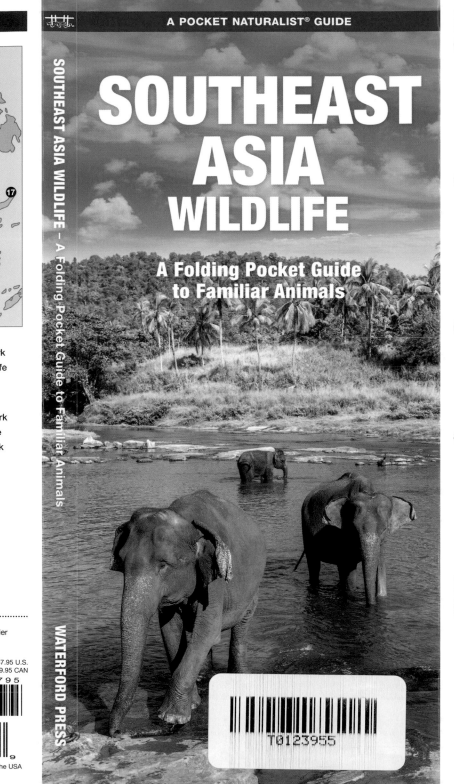

SOUTHEAST ASIA WILDLIFE

A Folding Pocket Guide to Familiar Animals

SOUTHEAST ASIA WILDLIFE – A Folding Pocket Guide to Familiar Animals

WATERFORD PRESS

T0123955

BUTTERFLIES & MOTHS

Common Rose
Pachliopta aristolochiae
To 4 in. (10 cm)

Tailed Jay
Graphium agamemnon
To 3 in. (8 cm)

Clipper
Parthenos sylvia
To 3.5 in. (9 cm)

Great Mormon
Papilio memnon
To 6 in. (15 cm)

Blue Glassy Tiger
Danaus vulgaris
To 3 in. (8 cm)

Common Mormon
Papilio polytes
To 4 in. (10 cm)

Paper Kite
Idea leuconoe
To 4 in. (10 cm)

Great Eggfly
Hypolimnas bolina
To 3.5 in. (9 cm)

Giant Orangetip
Hebomoia glaucippe
To 4 in. (10 cm)

Common Lime Butterfly
Papilio demoleus
To 4 in. (10 cm)

Malay Lacewing
Cethosia hypsea
To 3 in. (8 cm)

Atlas Moth
Attacus atlas
To 10 in. (25 cm)
Has the largest wing area of any moth.

Tropical Swallowtail Moth
Lyssa zampa
To 6 in. (15 cm)

Gaudy Baron
Euthalia lubentina
To 3 in. (8 cm)

Common Sailer
Neptis hylas
To 2 in. (5 cm)
Glides with wings held stiffly open.

REPTILES & AMPHIBIANS

Common Sun Skink
Eutropis multifasciata
To 14 in. (35 cm)

Tokay Gecko
Gekko gecko To 20 in. (50 cm)
Note large size. Named for its common, loud call -- tokay, to-kay.

Common House Gecko
Hemidactylus frenatus
To 6 in. (15 cm)

Asian Leaf Turtle
Cyclemys dentata
To 10 in. (25 cm)

Asian Horned Frog
Megophrys spp.
To 3.5 in. (9 cm)
Note elongate "eyebrows."

Common Gliding Lizard
Draco sumatranus
To 7 in. (18 cm)
One of several species of lizards. It is capable of gliding between trees for distances up to 200 ft. (60 m).

Reticulated Python
Python reticulatus
To 23 ft. (7 m)
The world's longest snake.

Elephant Trunk Snake
Acrochordus javanicus
To 8 ft. (2.4 m)
Baggy-skinned, aquatic snake is also called wart snake.

Flying Snake
Chrysopelea spp. To 4 ft. (1.2 m)
Arboreal snake has the ability to flatten its body and glide long distances.

Tentacled Snake
Erpeton tentaculatum
To 30 in. (75 cm)
Has fleshy, tentacle-like structures on its face.
Venomous, aquatic snake.

Mangrove Snake
Boiga dendrophila
To 8 ft. (2.4 m)

Green Pit Viper
Trimeresurus albolabris
To 2 ft. (60 cm)
Venomous.

Banded Sea Krait
Laticauda colubrina
To 56 in. (1.4 m)
Venomous, aquatic snake.

Burmese Python
Python molurus bivittatus
To 19 ft. (5.7 m)

REPTILES & AMPHIBIANS

Komodo Dragon
Varanus komodoensis
To 10 ft. (3 m)
The largest of several species of monitor lizard found in SE Asia.

King Cobra
Ophiophagus hannah
To 19 ft. (5.7 m)
Color ranges from greenish to black. Note light yellow crossbands along body. Is the largest venomous snake in the world.

Saltwater Crocodile
Crocodylus porosus To 20 ft. (6 m)
The largest living reptile is found in coastal saltwater lagoons, estuaries and swamps. Weighs up to 2,200 lbs. (1000 kg).

BIRDS

Little Cormorant
Microcarbo niger
To 20 in. (50 cm)

Gray Heron
Ardea cinerea
To 38 in. (95 cm)

Little Heron
Butorides striatus
To 14 in. (35 cm)
Note black cap.

Black-crowned Night Heron
Nycticorax nycticorax
To 28 in. (70 cm)

Great Egret
Ardea alba
To 38 in. (95 cm)
Note yellow bill and black feet.

Cattle Egret
Bubulcus ibis
To 20 in. (50 cm)

Little Egret
Egretta garzetta
To 26 in. (65 cm)
Note black bill and yellow feet.

Common Pintail
Anas acuta
To 30 in. (75 cm)

Little Grebe
Tachybaptus ruficollis
To 12 in. (30 cm)
Also called dabchick.

Lesser Whistling-Duck
Dendrocygna javanica
To 16 in. (40 cm)

BIRDS

Black Kite
Milvus migrans
To 22 in. (55 cm)

Black-shouldered Kite
Elanus caeruleus
To 14 in. (35 cm)
Note all-white tail.

Osprey
Pandion haliaetus
To 2 ft. (60 cm)
Fish-eating raptor.

Crested Serpent Eagle
Spilornis cheela
To 30 in. (75 cm)
Note black head crest.

Shikra
Accipiter badius
To 12 in. (30 cm)

Brahminy Kite
Haliastur indus
To 19 in. (48 cm)

Eurasian Kestrel
Falco tinnunculus
To 12 in. (30 cm)

Crested Wood-Partridge
Rollulus rouloul
To 10 in. (25 cm)

Common Gallinule
Gallinula chloropus
To 14 in. (35 cm)

Red Junglefowl
Gallus gallus
To 30 in. (75 cm)

Red-wattled Lapwing
Vanellus indicus
To 14 in. (35 cm)

Purple Swamphen
Porphyrio porphyrio
To 18 in. (45 cm)

White-breasted Waterhen
Amaurornis phoenicurus
To 13 in. (33 cm)

Pheasant-tailed Jacana
Hydrophasianus chirurgus
To 23 in. (58 cm)

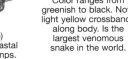

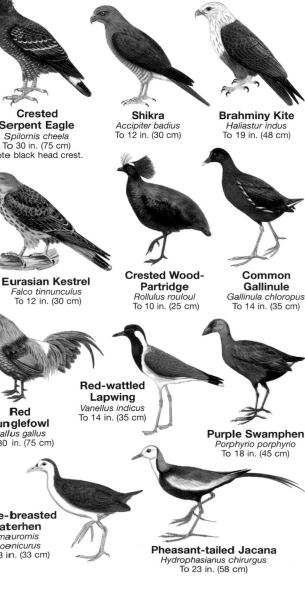

Greater Flameback
Chrysocolaptes guttacristatus
To 13 in. (33 cm)

White-throated Fantail
Rhipidura albicollis To 8 in. (20 cm)
Active and restless, it fans its tail when perching.

Asian Glossy Starling
Aplonis panayensis
To 8 in. (20 cm)

Blue-tailed Bee-eater
Merops philippinus
To 12 in. (30 cm)

Blue-throated Bee-eater
Merops viridis
To 11 in. (28 cm)

Common Kingfisher
Alcedo atthis
To 7 in. (18 cm)

White-throated Kingfisher
Halcyon smyrnensis
To 9 in. (23 cm)

Coppersmith Barbet
Megalaima haemacephala
To 7 in. (18 cm)
Repetitive call – *tuk-tuk-tuk* – has been likened to a hammer striking metal.

Pink-necked Green Pigeon
Treron vernans
To 10 in. (25 cm)

Asian Koel
Eudynamys scolopaceus
To 18 in. (45 cm)
Note red eyes.

Scaly-breasted Munia
Lonchura punctulata
To 4 in. (10 cm)

Rock Pigeon
Columba livia
To 13 in. (33 cm)

Spotted Dove
Spilopelia chinensis
To 13 in. (33 cm)
Note white-spotted black collar on neck.

Zebra Dove
Geopelia striata
To 8 in. (20 cm)

Red-whiskered Bulbul
Pycnonotus jocosus
To 7 in. (18 cm)

Black-naped Blue Monarch
Hypothymis azurea
To 6 in. (15 cm)

House Crow
Corvus splendens
To 16 in. (40 cm)

Pacific Swallow
Hirundo tahitica
To 5 in. (13 cm)

Common Iora
Aegithina tiphia
To 6 in. (15 cm)

Black-naped Oriole
Oriolus chinensis
To 11 in. (28 cm)

Oriental Magpie-Robin
Copsychus saularis
To 7.5 in. (19 cm)

Wreathed Hornbill
Rhyticeros undulatus
To 40 in. (1 m)

Great Hornbill
Buceros bicornis
To 42 in. (1.1 m)

Common Tailorbird
Orthotomus sutorius
To 5.5 in. (14 cm)
Familiar backyard species.

Common Myna
Acridotheres tristis
To 9 in. (23 cm)

Indian Roller
Coracias benghalensis
To 11 in. (28 cm)

Black Drongo
Dicrurus macrocercus
To 11 in. (28 cm)
Note white spot near beak.

Eurasian Tree Sparrow
Passer montanus
To 6 in. (15 cm)

Greater Coucal
Centropus sinensis
To 19 in. (48 cm)

Common Treeshrew
Tupaia glis
To 18 in. (45 cm)
Note pointed nose.

Large Flying Fox
Pteropus vampyrus
To 16 in. (40 cm)
Large, dog-faced bat has a wingspan of up to 5 ft. (1.5 m)

Moon Rat
Echinosorex gymnura
To 28 in. (70 cm)
Nocturnal species smells strongly of ammonia.

Tri-colored Squirrel
Callosciurus spp.
To 2 ft. (60 cm)
There are 15 distinct species in this genus.

Banded Linsang
Prionodon linsang
To 30 in. (75 cm)

Flying Lemur
Cynocephalus spp.
To 2 ft. (60 cm)
Does not fly but glides between trees. Also called colugo.

Hog-Badger
Arctonyx collaris
To 35 in. (88 cm)
Found in forested areas.

Malayan Porcupine
Hystrix brachyura
To 33 in. (83 cm)

Sunda Pangolin
Manis javanica To 4 ft. (1.2 m)
Body is covered with large scales. Curls into a ball when threatened.

Palm Civet
Paradoxurus spp. To 40 in. (1 m)
The expensive coffee kopi luwak is produced with beans that are eaten and excreted by palm civets.

Binturong
Arctictis binturong To 5 ft. (1.5 m)
Large weasel-like mammal has a prehensile tail. Also called bearcat.

Oriental Small-clawed Otter
Aonyx cinerea
To 40 in. (1 m)
The smallest otter species in the world weighs less than 5 lbs. (2.3 kg).

Dhole
Cuon alpinus
To 5 ft. (1.5 m)
Also called Indian wild dog. Endangered.

Golden Jackal
Canis aureus To 40 in. (1 m)
Note dark tip on tail.

Sloth Bear
Melursus ursinus To 6 ft. (1.8 m)
Has a long, shaggy coat, pale muzzle and white claws. Feeds primarily on ants and termites.

Red Panda
Ailurus fulgens To 4 ft. (1.2 m)
Is the only living species of the family Alluridae; it was previously classified as both a bear and a raccoon.

Asiatic Black Bear
Ursus thibetanus To 6 ft. (1.8 m)
Feeds on plants and on animals as big as water buffaloes. Also called moon bear for its U-shaped chest patch.

Sun Bear
Helarctos malayanus To 5 ft. (1.5 m)
Has large, yellowish sun-shaped patch on neck. Feeds primarily on insects and fruit and small animals.

Jungle Cat
Felis chaus To 50 in. (1.3 m)
Note tufted ears, leg stripes.

Fishing Cat
Prionailurus viverrinus
To 26 in. (65 cm)
Feeds primarily on fish it scoops out of the water with its paws.

Tiger
Panthera tigris To 12 ft. (3.6 m)
Three subspecies are found in SE Asia – the Sumatran, Malayan and Indochinese tiger. Endangered.

Asian Golden Cat
Catopuma temminckii
To 42 in. (1.1 m)
Coat colors range from golden to black.

Leopard Cat
Prionailurus bengalensis
To 3 ft. (90 cm)

Marbled Cat
Pardofelis marmorata To 26 in. (65 cm)
Lives in trees and feeds primarily on birds.

Crab-eating Macaque
Macaca fascicularis
To 4 ft. (1.2 m)
Also called the long-tailed macaque.

White-handed Gibbon
Hylobates lar
To 20 in. (50 cm)

Tarsier
Family Tarsius
To 15 in. (38 cm)
Small nocturnal primate has large eyes.

Rhesus Macaque
Macaca mulatta
To 30 in. (75 cm)
Common near human settlements.

Southern Pig-tailed Macaque
Macaca nemestrina
To 30 in. (75 cm)
Short tail is held erect.

Silvery Lutung
Trachypithecus cristatus
To 5 ft. (1.5 m)
Long-tailed monkey lacks a prehensile tail. Dark, gray-tipped coat has a silvery appearance.

Proboscis Monkey
Nasalis larvatus To 30 in. (75 cm)
Males have a long, pendulous nose. Endemic to Borneo.

Slow Loris
Nycticebus spp. To 15 in. (38 cm)
Nocturnal, arboreal primate has large eyes and a stocky build.

Siamang
Symphalangus syndactylus
To 5 ft. (1.5 m)
Has a large throat pouch it inflates to make loud calls. Endangered.

Orangutan
Pongo spp. To 6 ft. (1.8 m)
Found in Borneo and Sumatra. The only great ape found in Asia.

Wild Boar
Sus scrofa To 6 ft. (1.8 m)
Introduced species.

Bearded Pig
Sus barbatus
To 5 ft. (1.5 m)

Malayan Tapir
Tapirus indicus
To 8 ft. (2.4 m)

Sambar Deer
Rusa unicolor To 10 ft. (3 m)
Huge deer has a shaggy coat. Males have large, forked antlers.

Barking Deer
Muntiacus spp.
To 21 in. (53 cm)
Also called Indian muntjac, it makes a bark-like call upon spotting a threat.

Sumatran Rhinoceros
Dicerorhinus sumatrensis
To 12 ft. (3.6 m)
The smallest rhinoceros species. Critically endangered.

Water Buffalo
Bubalus spp. To 52 in. (1.3 m) H
Weighs up to 2,200 lbs. (1000 kg).

Gaur
Bos gaurus To 14 ft. (4.2 m)
Massive bovid has large ears and curved horns. Weighs up to 3,300 lbs. (1500 kg). Also called Indian bison.

Dugong
Dugong dugon
To 11 ft. (3.3 m)
Lives in shallow coastal waters.

Asian Elephant
Elephas maximus
To 11.5 ft. (3.5 m) H
Its dome shaped head and smaller ears differentiate it from the African elephant. Only male Asian elephants have tusks.

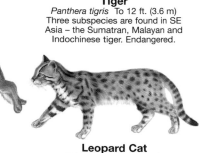
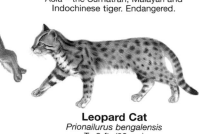